TO JESUS
THROUGH MARY

FR. AZAM 'VIANNEY' MANSHA, CJM
EUDIST PRIEST - MISSIONARY OF MERCY

ISBN: 978-1-959312-25-3

Copyright ©2025, by
The Eudists – CJM, Inc.
All Rights Reserved.

Published by

PO Box 3619
Vista, CA 92085

www.eudistsusa.org

This book is dedicated to my parents (Mansha Masih and Surriya Bibi), my grandparents (Sharif Masih and Meera Bibi), and Fathers Augustine Soares, Robert D'Silva & Pierre Drouin.

TABLE OF CONTENTS

Chapter 1
    Fr. Azam - Beginning a Journey with the Eudist Fathers 1
    The Marian Journey of St. John Eudes (1601-1680) 4
        A Miraculous Birth 4
        The Blessed Virgin Mary's Intercession 5
        The Blessed Virgin Mary and the Congregations.................. 6
        The Admirable Heart of Mary 7
        Mary and the Missions 10
        Mary and Eudes' Trials 11
        John Eudes' Contract with Mary: "A Covenant of Marriage" 12
        Mary and Eudes' Last Will 13

Chapter 2
    Fr. Azam - Turning Toward Mary 15
    Eudist Marian Spirituality 17
        The Symbolic Meaning of The Heart of Mary 18
        The Heart of Mary: Turning Toward Jesus Christ 19

Chapter 3
    What is the Marian School?... 21
    Eudist Marian Statue 25
    Fr. Azam - My Parents' Wedding Ring 26

About Saint John Eudes 27

About the Eudist Family 31

About the Author 35

Endnotes 37

CHAPTER 1
TO JESUS THROUGH MARY

FR. AZAM - BEGINNING A JOURNEY WITH THE EUDIST FATHERS

It was the year 2014, and I was a fourth-year, second semester theology student in Pakistan. I was already dreaming about my priestly ordination. My aunty, who is a Good Shepherd nun, was in Sri Lanka, and she was planning with my family to buy my ordination chasuble. All was going well, and I was grateful to the Lord for all things.

But one day the new archbishop of my diocese called me into his offi ce and told me to discontinue my priestly formation. He did not give me any reason and just told me that it was the decision of the council. I had been in the seminary for ten long years, but everything came to an abrupt end in 10 minutes. During my years of formation, I had always believed —and still believe— that the Church is a loving Mother, but my belief was shattered by this hurtful experience, and I found myself questioning how a mother could do this to her own child. But I decided to accept the decision as part of God's plan for me, even as I went home broken and wounded.

I told my elder brother about the archdiocesan decision. For his part, my brother smiled at me and said, "Welcome home." Meanwhile, it took me almost three weeks before I could break the news to my mother. To my shock, she not only cried with me, but she also smiled at me and said, "Stay with me! One day you will be a good priest." (I am already a priest, but still in the process of becoming a good priest).

The news of my formation discontinuance broke out among our relatives. One of them approached my mother to ask if I was willing to get married. Apart from the seemingly humorous timing of the proposition, I did find myself open to the thought of getting married.

I was also happy with the notion of this arranged marriage because my "intended" spouse was a doctoral student in sociology, and I was planning to resume and finish my advanced studies. It seemed to be a "perfect match," to say the least.

But one day, out of the blue, my spiritual director, Fr. Robert D'Silva (may his soul rest in peace) called and asked for me to visit him. Those who are spiritual directors here know that directors do not often call a directee; they wait until the directee approaches them. But my spiritual director was unique in the sense that he was the type who would call me if I did not see him for two months in a row. He was my spiritual director for 9 years.

Fr. Robert D'Silva was a man who left his high-fl ying army career to become a priest. He was a pastor of my native parish, St. Anthony of Padua in Karachi, for many years. He knew me from childhood. Throughout parish life and seminary formation, I always looked up to him for inspiration, encouragement, and guidance. So, when Fr. Robert called me, I was not able to say NO. I went and told him the sad news. We both cried and cried!!! After some time, he asked me what I intended to do. I told him that I had accepted the decision of my archbishop and had taken it as God's decision for me. I also told him that I was planning to get married and even asked him if he could preside over the wedding Mass.

But in his wisdom, he gently told me that superiors are also human beings, and that they, too, can make mistakes in their decision. He went on to say that "our Church is human and divine." He ended our conversation by telling me, "Therefore I believe you should try somewhere else." To tell you the truth, I was reluctant to do so, but I could not find it in myself to refuse Fr. Robert, because I had always regarded him as a man of God, a spiritual father, and my soul's director, standing *in persona Christi* to me, so I said YES to him.

The next day, I drafted an email to almost thirty congregations, and to my surprise twenty-six congregations replied within the same day, expressing their willingness to initiate the process of dialogue and discernment. It was a sure and visible sign for me that God was still calling me to the priestly vocation.

I was not sure what God had planned for me, so I went on a Marian pilgrimage to seek her powerful intercession. Indeed, it brought calmness and enthusiasm to me, but again I wondered where should I go? What direction should I take? Once again, I turned towards the

Blessed Virgin Mary and asked her powerful intercession, so that I could serve her Only Son - Jesus Christ. There was an inner voice in me that said, "go for a discernment retreat."

So, I went on an Ignatian retreat to help deepen my discernment and hopefully come to the right decision. Receiving so many affirmative responses from congregations in the United States, Ireland, England, and France only added to my uncertainty and befuddlement. Even after my retreat, I still was not able to decide where to go. While immersed in this mental and spiritual quandary, I went to see my aunty, Sr. Maqsood Ambrose, who is a Sister of Our Lady of Charity of the Good Shepherd. Upon seeing me, she immediately asked me: "So when are you going to write to the Eudist Fathers?" I took her words as the voice of God, cutting straight through my confused mind and directing my steps towards the Eudist Fathers in the Philippines.

It was the Will of God that I needed to be sent out of my own diocese. It was the Will of God that I joined the Eudist Fathers, and it is the Will of God that today I am speaking to you. If I had not been sent out from my own diocese, I would not have gone to the Philippines, and if I had not gone to the Philippines, I could not have become a Eudist Priest, and if I were not a Eudist, how could I write this book?!

The Marian Journey of St. John Eudes (1601-1680)

On Wednesday, November 14, 1601, a child was born in the family of Isaac and Martha Eudes. He was baptized with the name of John on Friday, November 16, in the church of Our Lady at Ri, France.[1] He entered the Oratory of Cardinal Pierre de Berulle[2] on March 25, 1623, and received the sacrament of Holy Orders on December 20, 1625. He celebrated his first Mass on Christmas Day of 1625 in the House of the Oratory in Paris on *Rue St. Honore*.[3] He remained nearly twenty years as an Oratorian, and then at the end of March 1643, he withdrew from that Congregation to start one of his own.

While an Oratorian, he founded the Order of the Sisters of Our Lady of Charity of the Refuge in 1641. Leaving the Oratorians, he founded the priestly Congregation of Jesus and Mary on March 25, 1643. He also founded a special society for laypeople: the Children of the Holy Heart of the Admirable Mother.[4]

St. John Eudes has made a distinctive contribution in the theological, liturgical, and devotional practices of Mariology, particularly his treatment of the Holy Heart of Mary. The first solemn public Mass in the world to honor the Holy Heart of Mary was composed and celebrated by St. John Eudes on February 8, 1648, in Autun, France.[5] He is also the first priest who dedicated a church in honor of the Heart of Mary.

While reflecting on the events of his life, St. John Eudes considered that he had been especially graced by Jesus Christ through the intercession of the Blessed Virgin Mary, to whom he had great devotion. The rest of this chapter will highlight the role of the Blessed Virgin Mary in the life of St. John Eudes and his devotion towards her.

A Miraculous Birth

Regarding his birth, St. John Eudes acknowledged that his parents did not have children for three years. They made a pilgrimage to the shrine of Our Lady of Recovery, eighteen miles from Ri. They prayed there to have a child and made a promise to Our Lady that they would offer the child to Our Lord and Our Lady.[6] St. John Eudes wrote in his *Memoriale Beneficiorum Dei*:

> My father and mother were married three years without being able to have children, because of a curse that had been cast upon them which prevented it. Then they made a vow, in honor of the Blessed Virgin, to go to Our Lady of Recovery, which is a place of devotion to this same Virgin in a chapel in the parish of Tourailles in the diocese of Seez. Afterwards, my mother then being pregnant, she and my father made a pilgrimage to the same chapel, where they offered and consecrated me to Our Lord and Our Lady.
>
> If doctors are correct in their opinion which holds that the soul is infused into the bodies of male children the fortieth day after conception, my soul was created by God and united with my body on the 25th of March, the day on which the Son of God was made incarnate and the Blessed Virgin Mary became the Mother of God. For I was born on the 14th of November, and consequently, having been conceived nine months previously, the 14th of February was the day of my conception. Now, from that day to the 25th of March there are exactly forty days.[7]

For his parents' pilgrimage to Our Lady of Recovery and their seeking the intercession of Mary, St. John Eudes expressed his gratitude to God for the blessing of religious parents. This act of gratitude he expressed in the following words: "God granted me the grace to be born of parents who were in a modest condition of life, who lived in holy fear of God, and who, I have every reason to believe, died in His grace and love."[8]

THE BLESSED VIRGIN MARY'S INTERCESSION

St. John Eudes always recognized the intercession of the Blessed Virgin Mary in his life. He experienced that she never left him alone in the difficult moments of his life. He constantly sought the intercession of Our Lady and received grace from Jesus Christ. St. John Eudes acknowledged:

> God preserved me many times through the intercession of my most kind Mother, the Blessed Virgin Mary, when I found myself on the verge of losing His grace and falling into the hell of sin.[9]

While experiencing the maternal love of Mary, he encouraged others to also seek the maternal intercession and comfort of the Blessed Virgin Mary. He wrote to a nun who was the eldest daughter of Monsieur Blouet de Camilly, who died in October 1661, that:

> Since Jesus is your spouse, my very dear daughter, the Mother of Jesus is your Mother. Throw yourself then at her feet in order to greet her and honor her in this relationship to you, and in order to offer and give yourself to her, swearing that you wish to serve her, love her, and follow her as your most good Mother, and begging her to protect, bless and guide you as her dear daughter. And say to her for these intentions, with all your heart: *Monstra te esse matrem*, "Show yourself a mother."[10]

THE BLESSED VIRGIN MARY AND THE CONGREGATIONS

On December 8, 1641, on the occasion of the Feast of Our Lady's Immaculate Conception, St. John Eudes opened a house of refuge for victims of human trafficking, which he dedicated to the Sacred Heart of Jesus. He founded an order of nuns to care for them, under the patronage of Our Lady. He called them the Sisters of Our Lady of Charity of the Refuge. The aim of this order, from its birth, was to provide residential care and guidance in the conversion and rehabilitation of women who had been trapped into lives as sex workers.[11] He wrote:

> It was also in 1641 that God granted me the grace of beginning the establishment of the house of Our Lady of Charity, on the day of the Immaculate Conception of the most Holy Mary.[12]

In 1651, the Order of the Sisters of Our Lady of Charity of the Refuge received recognition from the King of France and national ecclesiastical authorities in Paris.[13] Cardinal Richelieu sent a letter-patent, authorizing these nuns to carry on their ministry to the women in need. The letter-patent was signed by the king at Saint Germain-en-Laye in November 1642, and the text states:

> ... under the invocation of Our Lady of Refuge, for the reception of two classes of persons, to wit: girls and women, who after having led a scandalous life, wish to retire there for some time, amend their conduct, with liberty to leave when they choose; also ladies of unsullied fame, who are perfectly free, and moved by the desire of serving God and working for the salvation of souls, voluntarily seclude themselves in the same house...[14]

Besides the Order of the Sisters Our Lady of Charity of the Refuge, in the same year (1641), Fr. Eudes worked to establish a Congregation of priests. The purpose was to form future priests and good laborers for the Gospel. He said:

> In 1641, during the octave of the Nativity of the Blessed Virgin Mary, God gave me the grace to formulate the plan of establishing our Congregation.[15]

At the age of 41, on leaving the Oratory of Cardinal Pierre de Berulle, St. John Eudes on March 25, 1643, Our Lady's Day of Annunciation, gathered five priests and took them on a pilgrimage to the shrine of the Blessed Virgin Mary at the Chapel of Notre Dame de la Delivrande, eight miles away from Caen. There at the chapel they prostrated themselves before Our Lady's statue and consecrated themselves to Jesus and Mary. The new Congregation came into existence with two chief objectives: the sanctification of the clergy and the evangelizing of the people of God through preaching parish missions.[16]

> In the year 1643, Our Lord and His most Holy Mother, in their excessive goodness, granted us the grace to begin the establishment of our little Congregation on March 25th, the day on which the Son of God was made man and the Blessed Virgin became the Mother of God.[17]

THE ADMIRABLE HEART OF MARY[18]

After establishing the community of priests, he received permission from Bishop d'Angennes to celebrate the Feast of Our Lady's Heart privately in his community chapel. The date he initially proposed to the bishop was October 20, but after some contemplation, he decided to celebrate it on February 8. To create the liturgical celebration in honor of the Admirable Heart of Mary, he prepared an office and composed the Holy Mass.[19] Through his great effort, preaching, and writings, the first solemn public Mass in the world in honor of Our Lady's Holy Heart was celebrated on February 8, 1648 in Autun, France.[20] Shortly before his death on August 19, 1680, St. John Eudes completed his masterpiece, *The Admirable Heart of the Most Holy Mother of God*. He took eighteen years to complete the book. One can see the book as an expression of his gratitude to Our Lady.

> July 25th of the same year 1680, God granted me the grace to finish my book, *The Admirable Heart of the Most Holy Mother of God*.[21]

The 20th century archbishop of Boston, Richard J. Cushing, said about the above-mentioned book of St. John Eudes, "This was the first book written on the devotion to the Sacred Hearts . . . one of the great devotional treatises which have shaped the history of Catholic prayer life." Further he said, "St. John Eudes [was] the 'prodigy of his time' and among his books none more enrich the spiritual lives of its readers than this incomparable devotional classic, *The Admirable Heart of Mary*."[22]

During the life of St. John Eudes, there were other people who appreciated and acknowledged his efforts to promote devotion to the Heart of Mary. Among them were the bishops who approved the office and liturgical celebration of the feast of the Heart of Mary in their respective dioceses, such as: Autun, Noyon, Lisieux, Coutances, Evreux, and Caen. In 1667 while conducting a mission at Evreux, St. John Eudes received permission from the bishop to establish the feast of the Most Holy Heart of the Blessed Virgin in this diocese as well. Fr. Eudes wrote:

> In 1667. . . During this mission we established the feast of the Most Holy Heart of the Blessed Virgin in several of the churches of Evreux, and His Lordship [the Bishop] granted permission for this to be done throughout his diocese.[23]

The Marian Journey of St. John Eudes (1601-1680)

Besides the diocesan bishops, there were two theologians, Dom de la Dangie de Renchy and Father Chancerel, who also approved the prayer *Ave Cor* written by St. John Eudes. The prayer *Ave Cor* was originally composed by St. Mechtilde, a follower of St. Gertrude. Fr. Eudes amplified it and composed it anew. It ran as follows:

Hail, Heart most holy.	We praise you,
Hail, Heart most meek.	We glorify you,
Hail, Heart most humble.	We give you thanks,
Hail, Heart most pure.	We love you, With all our hearts,
Hail, Heart most devout.	With all our soul,
Hail, Heart most wise.	With all our strength;
Hail, Heart most patient.	We offer you our heart, We give it to you,
Hail, Heart most obedient.	
Hail, Heart most vigilant.	We consecrate it to you, We sacrifice,
Hail, Heart most faithful.	
Hail, Heart most blessed.	Receive it and possess it entirely,
Hail, Heart most merciful.	Purify it, Enlighten it, and Sanctify it.
Hail, most loving Heart of Jesus and Mary:	In it live and reign now and forever.
We adore you,	Amen.[24]

A Jesuit from Canada, Fr. Pierre Joseph Marie Chaumonot wrote a letter of appreciation to Fr. Eudes for his efforts, devotion, and love for Mary. He wanted to unite with St. John Eudes and learn from him about the Admirable Heart of Mary. The text in the letter goes like this:

> . . . Might I dare to ask of you, for the love of Mary, Virgin and Mother, whom you so much love, to procure for me the advantage of being admitted, as the last of your servitors to the service of this Sovereign Mistress . . . as much as it is in our power, to beg a part of the devotion which you have for her . . . I should be glad to learn that there is an association of *Chaplains of Our Lady* . . . honoring the Blessed Virgin, and of offering to God, by Her hands her adorable Son . . . please begin this association, and do me the favor to admit me to it . . . The love which you have for the Blessed Virgin serves me as an excuse

for having taken the liberty to write to you so familiarly, I, who am only a poor man whom nobody knows.[25]

Mary and the Missions[26]

St. John Eudes carried a particular Marian image on his 117 missions, pictured on pg. 24 of this book.[27] Robert de Pas writes: *"it was a small statue in stuccoed and polychrome wood. This statue belonged to Saint John Eudes; it was on his table, and he sometimes took it on his missions."*[28] During his missions, he never forgot to thank Our Lady for all her intercessions for him before Jesus Christ. He acknowledged that through her intercession, he was able to receive many favors during different missions. To give honor to Our Lady he established and dedicated a church to the Holy Heart of Mary. This became the first church in the world which was named after the Heart of Mary.[29] He thanked Our Lady who granted him all the favors, and he wrote:

> I must not forget seven other favors bestowed upon us by Our Lord and His Holy Mother, for which I owe them particular thanks.
>
> ...The second favor was that Our Lord Jesus Christ and His most worthy Mother granted us the grace to erect a church in Coutances, over a period of three years. This is the first church ever to be built and dedicated in honor of the most Holy Heart of the Blessed Virgin, who has but one Heart with her beloved Son.
>
> ...The fourth was that, through a wonderful demonstration of His divine might and infinite mercy, God deigned to give us, contrary to all likelihood, the large square in front of our house in Caen for the construction of a church in honor of the most Holy Heart of our admirable Mother, and for the erection of the other building and accommodations we needed, availing Himself of His Lordship Francis Servien, the bishop of Bayeux to provide us this gift...
>
> The fifth is that God preserved me many times, through the intercession of the most kind Mother, the Blessed Virgin Mary,

when I found myself on the verge of losing His grace and falling into the hell of sin.

...The seventh is an infinite number of other graces that Our Lord has granted me, through the mediation of His most worthy Mother, for which may they both be blessed and glorified for all eternity.[30]

MARY AND EUDES' TRIALS

Our Lady never left her spiritual son St. John Eudes alone. As an example, the author would like to present only one of many incidents.[31] There were moments when St. John Eudes was in great difficulties. He needed to pay a large amount of money to the city government. He did not have any resources to pay. But through the intercession of Mary, the help arrived. He tells us:

> In the year 1662, on a Saturday, the eve of the Visitation of Our Lady, Our Lord provided us with the means of repaying a loan of three hundred sixty-nine livres which we had owed to the city of Caen for the square in front of our house which had been granted us in fief. . . out of pure charity he [a man from Paris who wishes to remain anonymous] or rather Our Lord and His most Holy Mother, gave us the sum of ten thousand francs, from which we took about eight thousand to effect this amortization and pay up two years of arrears owed on the aforesaid loan. Therefore, I dedicated and consecrated the square, on the same day, in honor of the most Holy Heart of the Blessed Virgin. I also made a vow to God, in the presence of the Blessed Sacrament, to recognize her as foundress of the church that we desired and hoped to later erect in that square in honor of this same Heart, as well as foundress of the houses necessary and expedient for our Community, and never to concede the title of founder or foundress to anyone else at all.[32]

JOHN EUDES' CONTRACT WITH MARY: "A COVENANT OF MARRIAGE"

On April 28, 1668, two years before his death, St. John Eudes wrote and signed a special contract, which can be described as a covenant of marriage, with the Most Blessed Mother of God. He wrote:

> Oh admirable and most amiable Mary, Mother of God, only Daughter of the eternal Father, Mother of the Son of God, Spouse of the Holy [Spirit], Queen of heaven and earth, it is no wonder thou art willing to be the spouse of the least of all men and greatest of all sinners . . . Oh most charitable of all creatures, deign to accept the conditions of our holy union which I am about to write down on this paper. It will serve as the contract, or rather, as a copy of the contract, of which I implore the Holy Spirit to be the notary, that He may record it in thy Heart and in mine in the golden and indelible letters of His pure love . . . I wish to respect and honor thee as my Queen and sovereign Lady, and I desire my whole being, with all its dependencies and appurtenances . . . in thanks for the numberless graces and favors which the heavenly Father has granted me through thy intercession . . . Oh my most honored Lady, that all that I am, all of which I am capable, all that I possess in body and soul, nature and grace, all that I hope for in glory, and in general, all that belongs to me in either the spiritual or temporal order, or that depends on me in any way whatsoever, be thine entirely and without reservation . . . Oh, had I a hundred million worlds, how gladly would I give them to thee, Oh my Holy Spouse! . . . I desire to dwell with thee in the most amiable Heart of Jesus, which is also thy Heart . . . Oh my all-desirable Queen, what do I wish, what do I love, in heaven and on earth, after thy Jesus and mine, other than thee! . . . I know there is nothing more pleasing to thy Son and thee than to labor for the salvation of souls . . .[33]

Eudes acknowledged that Our Lady is the Mother of Life and Grace as he wrote:

> Blessed are you, Oh Jesus, for all that you are and all that you accomplish in your most holy Mother! Blessed are you, Mary, for all the honor you have given your beloved Son throughout

The Marian Journey of St. John Eudes (1601-1680)

your entire life. I offer you all my life, Oh Mother of Life and Grace. With my whole heart, I beg your Son, Jesus, the God of life and love, to grant that my entire life may pay continual homage to His most holy life and yours.[34]

MARY AND EUDES' LAST WILL

St. John Eudes wrote in his last will and testament that he wished to be buried with specific Marian religious articles. The eloquence of his great love and devotion can be seen in the following text:

> I implore my dearest brethren to bury me in the little white habit of my loving Mother, including the while silk girdle and the heart bearing a red silk cross, as well as the alb I have marked for that purpose, together with the holy scapular, the holy rosary given me by Sister Mary des Vallees, the original of my last will and testament, of which this copy will survive, the *Contract of Marriage* that I made with the Blessed Virgin, and above all, the holy image which is fashioned in part from holy relics and is kept in a small niche of gilded copper. [35]

In the last moment of his life, St. John Eudes once again celebrated the love and devotion of Mary in the following words:

> . . . with all my heart do I give my soul, O Mother of love, in union with the same love by which my Savior gave thee His at the moment of His Incarnation. Do thou preserve it as something which is wholly thine; receive it into thy most sacred hands when it leaves my body, harbor it in thy maternal Heart; present and give it to thy beloved Son, that He may place it in the ranks of those who will love and bless Him for all eternity with thee and with all the angels and saints in that blessed eternity. "Oh clement, oh loving, oh sweet Virgin Mary, my life, my sweetness, and my dearest hope."[36]

St. John Eudes died on August 19, 1680. The Holy Mother Church appreciates his service and promotes the devotion of the Sacred Heart of Jesus and the Admirable Heart of Mary. Therefore, on May 31, 1909, Pius X inscribed him among the Blessed and Pope Pius XI canonized him in 1925. In their respective bulls of beatification and canonization, both pontiffs titled St. John Eudes "The Father, Doctor, and Apostle of Liturgical Devotion to the Sacred Heart of Jesus and Mary." Through an order of Pius XI, a statue of St. John Eudes was placed in the central nave of St. Peter's Basilica in Rome.[37]

CHAPTER 2

TO JESUS THROUGH MARY

FR. AZAM - TURNING TOWARD MARY

It was June 14, 2014, when all the arrangements were settled and I was all prepared to go to the Philippines! I had just received my passport and visa, the last two things I was waiting for, and finally, I allowed myself to get all excited to join the Eudists there. It was a fine afternoon, and I was having lunch with my family. With my flight still at 11:55 PM that night, I was able to enjoy our lunch as we shared memories about growing up.

Right after lunch, I gave my shoulder bag to my younger sister, asking her to be so kind as to wash it for me. Without me realizing that my passport was in it and without my sister checking if there were any valuables in it, she put my shoulder bag directly into the washing machine. By the time I realized that my passport was in it, it was too late. As a result, I wasn't able to travel that night, postponing my trip to the Philippines.

The very next day, I went to the passport office to get a new passport. One of the requirements was my national identification card, which unfortunately, I wasn't carrying with me at that time. I went back home to get it, but I couldn't find it! You know how it is with the things we lose in our house; we will only find them on judgment day! So, I went to the national database office to apply for a new national identity card, only to find out that there was a clerical mistake in my records. The officer said, "Your younger brother was born just three months after you!" In my heart, I said to myself, "Wow! Mama is a superwoman!" Now Mama didn't tell me about this and so I couldn't do anything but head back home with a broken heart.

When I got home, Mama looked at me and smiled. It seemed like she knew what was going on, but still, she asked me about things. I told her the whole story, and I said, "Mama, I don't know what's going on." She again smiled and told me, "Why don't you go to the Marian

15

shrine?" So, I headed for a special shrine in Punjab Lahore and ended up crying to our Blessed Mother.

While I was leaving the station on my way back to Karachi, I met this tall man who approached me, shook my hand, and started talking with me. He told me, "I like the way you preach, and I'd like you to visit my office." You know, when you're brokenhearted, you really don't want to talk to anybody. I worked hard to control my emotions, because as much as I didn't want to talk to him, I didn't want to be rude to him either. I ended up saying to him, "Sure, I'll visit your office." Deep in my heart though, I was looking for my passport. Now this tall man gave me his business card and asked me to come see him at his office. I took his card without even looking at his name on it, and I promised him that I would.

The very next day, the day I intended to visit him, I took his business card from my pocket. That was when I saw his name and I was shocked (name and designation are kept secret for privacy purposes). I was so shocked, and in my heart I said, "Oh, Mama works very fast!" And so, I went straight away to him. Upon arriving, his secretary wanted me to make an appointment. I tried to convince her to just inform the gentleman that I was there to see him, but she insisted that I make an appointment. I finally gave in, after which she said to come back after two weeks. I said, "No, I need to see him urgently." In the end, she understood my dilemma and said, "Okay, if Sir does not want to see you today, then you have to promise that you won't come back for two weeks." I said, "Okay."

She went inside to inform him. Later on, she told me that when she informed him that there was a young man named Azam waiting outside for him, he jumped from his chair and said, "Oh! That little man is here!" And so, he came out and invited me into his office. He offered me some tea, and I immediately took out my passport and gave it to him. I said, "Sir, I'm here for the renewal of my passport. I have a problem with it." He looked at me. He looked at my passport. He took my passport and gave it to his secretary.

As we waited, I shared with him the story about Lazarus who was dead for four days and how Jesus, with His powerful words, made Lazarus rise from the dead and brought him back to life. I was conversing with him for almost 30 minutes and started having tea with him. It was after some time that his secretary returned and handed me a brand-new passport! I was in complete shock, but I truly believed back then, as I believe now, that everything unfolded as it did because of the powerful intercession of the Blessed Mother Virgin Mary.

EUDIST MARIAN SPIRITUALITY

The 17th century French School of Spirituality[38] has made a significant contribution to Marian spirituality. One of the principle themes of the masters of the French School of Spirituality was Mariology.[39] One can say that Marian spirituality took a decisive step forward in the Catholic Church with the French School of Spirituality. Among these spiritual masters, St. John Eudes has made a distinctive contribution in the theological, liturgical, and devotional aspects of Mariology, particularly his treatment of the Heart of Mary.[40] It is through the efforts of St. John Eudes that the first public liturgical celebration was held in honor of the Heart of Mary in 1648 at Autun.[41] He was also the first priest to dedicate a church with the name of the Holy Heart of Mary in 1653 at Coutances. According to St. John Eudes, he had been graced in a unique way to have been given the Heart of Jesus and that of his most beloved mother Mary. He wrote in his Last Will and Testament:

> To the fullest extent of my will, I give myself to that incomprehensible love through which Jesus and my Mother of all goodness gave me their most lovable Heart in a very special way. In union with this same love, I bequeath this Heart as something which belongs to me and of which I can dispose for the glory of my God.[42]

In the writings of St. John Eudes, again according to Archbishop Cushing, *The Admirable Heart of the Mother of God* is the synthesis or a central treatise.[43] St. John Eudes completed this book just three months before his death in 1680. At his beatification St. Pius X called him "The Father, Doctor and Apostle of liturgical devotion to the Hearts of Jesus and Mary."[44]

THE SYMBOLIC MEANING OF THE HEART OF MARY

St. John Eudes was a man of Scripture and of deep contemplation. His devotional reflections were fully developed based on Sacred Scripture. Therefore, in his last book written prior to dying, when he explained the symbolic meaning of the Heart of Mary, he drew his interpretations for the meaning of the word "heart" from many places in Sacred Scripture, such as:

1. The memory, i.e., to remember what God has done in your life (Deut 6:4)
2. The intellect, i.e., reasoning on the things of God (Ps 18:15).
3. Free will, i.e., the mother of all virtue and of vice (Lk 6:45)
4. Seat of contemplation, i.e., turning the mind directly towards God.
5. The whole interior life of man, i.e., carrying the instructions in your heart as a mark of God (Song of Songs 8:6).[45]

St. John Eudes had learned from St. Augustine that before conceiving Jesus in her womb, Mary conceived him in her heart,[46] which according to St. John Eudes is "the heart of His Father, and the Holy Spirit, who is the heart of the Father and the Son." One can conclude here that for St. John Eudes, Mary did not receive Jesus only in her womb, but she received Jesus in her soul. He says: "Mary bore him in her womb for only nine months, but she carried him in her Heart from the very first moment of her life and will continue to carry him eternally."[47] St. John Eudes frequently meditated on two special Lucan texts that both say: "Mary kept all these things in her heart and pondered on them" (Luke 2:19 and 2:51). He writes:

> The Heart of the Blessed Virgin is the depository and faithful guardian of the marvelous mysteries of the Savior. She kept all the marvels of the life of her Son, in a way, in her bodily heart, the source of her life and the seat of all her impulses; all the movements and beats of her heart were for Jesus.

He goes on:

> She kept them in her heart, that is to say, in her memory, her intelligence, her will and in the deepest recesses of her mind, since all the faculties of her soul were ceaselessly applied to remembering, meditating, contemplating, adoring and glorifying all that was happening in the life of her Son.

He continues:

> She kept them in her Heart, according to the divine words: "Place me as a seal on your heart" (Song of Songs, 8:6); that is

to say, she focused on engraving in her soul and her interior life a perfect image of the holy life of her Son. She kept them in her Heart with the help of the Holy Spirit who is the spirit of her spirit, the heart of her Heart, who reminded her of these things to nourish her contemplation and relate them to the Apostles and disciples.[48]

He concludes:

> Indeed, this incomparable Heart of the Mother of our Redeemer is a flawless mirror in which Jesus, the Sun of eternity, is reflected perfectly, in all his beauty and perfections."[49]

It seems, for St. John Eudes that the Heart of Mary is a place where she received, pondered, and nourished Jesus prior to his birth and conception as well. Later she presented Jesus to the world, the savior of humanity, through a miraculous birth, beginning with Elizabeth and John the Baptist. Therefore, it is necessary to see the Heart of Mary as being continually full of tenderness, mercy, and compassion because Jesus is living there prior to and after his birth. St. John Eudes says,

> The Heart of Mary is Jesus himself, because Jesus lives and reigns so fully in Mary that he is the soul of her soul, the spirit of her spirit, and the heart of her heart.[50]

THE HEART OF MARY: TURNING TOWARD JESUS CHRIST

Marian devotion, according to St. John Eudes, is turning toward Jesus (Jn 2:3). Mary encourages the community of faithful to confidently bring their needs to her only son Jesus as she did at Cana: "they have no wine." Later, with the same confidence and trust in Jesus, she turns toward others and says, "Do whatever he tells you to do" (Jn 2:5). Marian devotion, according to St. John Eudes, is not a sentimental kind of devotional practice, but it is a real consecration to Jesus, i.e., to see Jesus in Mary and to see Mary in Jesus. He writes:

> Oh Jesus, only Son of God and Son of Mary, I contemplate and adore you living and reigning in your most holy Mother and as

the one who is all and does all in her. You are her life, her soul, her heart, her spirit, her treasure. You are in her, sanctifying her on earth and glorifying her in heaven. You are in her, clothing her with your qualities, imprinting in her a most perfect image of yourself.

Blessed are you, Oh Jesus, for all that you are and all that you accomplish in your most holy Mother! Blessed are you, Mary, for all the honor you have given your beloved Son throughout your entire life. I offer you all my life, Oh Mother of life and grace. With my whole heart, I beg your Son, Jesus, the God of life and love, to grant that my entire life may pay continual homage to his most holy life and yours.[51]

Mary cannot be separated from Jesus. She follows her Son during his ministry (Luke 11). She believes in her Son prior to his first sign and continues to believe in him after the first sign in Cana (Jn 2:1-11). These actions of Mary, according to St. John Eudes, mark her as "the incomparable Virgin Mary, chosen from among all creatures to be His [Jesus'] Mother." Therefore, when a believer has a Marian devotion, for St. John Eudes it is no "greater service to Jesus Christ to do anything more pleasing to Him [Jesus] than to serve and honor His most worthy Mother."[52]

CHAPTER 3

TO JESUS THROUGH MARY

THE MARIAN SCHOOL

St. John Eudes is known for his Marian devotion. Since 1641, he worked on the liturgical text for the Mass and Divine Office for a feast in honor of the Immaculate Heart of Blessed Virgin Mary (IHBVM). For seven years (1641 to 1648), he celebrated the Mass in the honor of IHBVM, but only privately. Through his hard work of preaching and writing on this feast, for the first time a public Mass was celebrated in the honor of IHBVM on February 8, 1648. In later years and prior to his death, Fr. Eudes explained the importance of and need for the Marian devotion in a book called *The Admirable Heart of Mary*.

This book is considered a synthesis of all the spiritual teachings of St. Eudes. According to Archbishop Richard J. Cushing, "The characteristic gifts of the devout writer, his elevation of thought and directness of expression, are admirably exemplified in the beloved pages of his Marian masterpiece."[53] St. John Eudes' devotion to the Sacred Heart of Jesus and Holy Heart of Mary led Pope Leo XIII to proclaim him the "Author... of liturgical devotion to the Sacred Heart of Jesus and Holy Heart of Mary."[54] This present chapter is an approach to understanding the Marian School according to St. John Eudes in the light of the exegetical meaning of John 19:25-27.

WHAT IS THE MARIAN SCHOOL?

The Marian School for St. John Eudes is "...a continuation of [Jesus'] life."[55] It is a place where Mary teaches a believer to see her only Son Jesus through her eyes, therefore it is important to be in the Marian School. Pope St. John Paul II also recommended this, "[Mary] was a unique witness to the mystery of Jesus. From the very first moment, the Church 'looked' at Mary through Jesus, as she 'looked' at Jesus through Mary."[56]

St. John Eudes learned from St. Augustine of Hippo that Jesus is the Word, Creator and Maker of His own mother. He created his own mother in order to be conceived in her.[57] For St. John Eudes, Jesus not only created his own mother but he also gave his mother to us through the Beloved Disciple. He says:

> She loves us with the same love with which she loves her Son, Jesus. She sees and loves us as her own children, since our Savior on the Cross gave us to his mother as her children, saying to each one of us what he said to the beloved disciple: 'Behold your Mother.'[58]

The Marian school, according to St. John Eudes, is "Beholding his mother." It is from the Cross that Jesus created a new family where Mary is the mother of all believers.[59] The Beloved Disciple obediently accepted the words of Jesus along with accepting Mary, the Mother of Jesus.[60] By accepting the words of Jesus, Mary and the Beloved Disciple enter into a new relationship, of mother and son:

> In John 19:25-27, Jesus makes known to his mother that the Beloved Disciple is her son and to the Disciple that she is his mother. Her silent agreement to become one of the Beloved Disciple's own indicates her obedience to the word of her Son.[61]

By accepting the words of Jesus, the mother of Jesus and the Beloved Disciple are now connected by their common faith and relationship with Jesus. Their mutual acceptance forms the nucleus of a new community of believers,[62] where disciples of Jesus become Jesus' brothers and sisters.[63] The Beloved Disciple has a unique relationship with Mary now, because he is moved into the place of Jesus as the son of Mary.[64] Conversely, in terms of faith in Jesus, a new familial relationship emerges. Mary and the Beloved Disciple have understood the words of Jesus. Mary accepts the maternal role in the new family of Jesus established at the Cross.[65] Feuillet comments, "Jesus transposes into a messianic and supernatural realm the maternal role of woman: of Mary first of all."[66]

In summarizing the above findings, we can conclude that the Marian School according to St. John Eudes is:

i. To behold the mother of Jesus, i.e., accepting the Mother of Jesus as one's own mother, which means entering into a unique relationship with Mary.
ii. To be a son and daughter of Mary, i.e., having been spiritually born from the same Mary in which Jesus was physically formed through the action of the Holy Spirit.
iii. To be a brother or sister of Jesus, i.e., sharing a close relationship with Jesus who happily has accepted believers as the spiritual children of Mary as well as his brothers and sisters.

To Jesus Through Mary

Eudist Marian Statue

St. John Eudes had a special Marian statue that he carried with him throughout his 117 missions. Robert de Pas writes "it was a small statue of stuccoed and polychrome wood. This statue belonged to St. John Eudes; it was on his table, and he sometimes took it with him on his missions."[67] Today this Marian image is found in the chapel of the Sisters of Our Lady of Charity of the Good Shepherd in Caen, France.

This traditional Marian Eudist statue has always fascinated me. It reminds me of God's promise made in many contexts (Leviticus 26:12; Exodus 34:10; Isaiah 7:14; Matthew 1:23; and Luke 1:31). In the New Testament, this promise was fulfilled, and a virgin conceived the Son of God (Luke 1:31-33). What a joy to know that the Divine has entered human history, as the evangelist says in the prologue to the fourth gospel "The Word became flesh and lived among us" (Jn 1:4).

It is the great humility of the Divine Son that chose the Virgin Mary to be His mother. It is magnificent to see that the child Jesus, who is the Lord of lords and the Messiah, feeds from his mother's breasts. In this statue, I see a fullness of love. A mother doesn't think of the world while feeding a child, while her son is not worried by the noise. A baby is happy to receive milk. Both mother and son are immersed in sharing their love, that is, the divine touching the human and the human touching the divine. She is blessed by Jesus, who was conceived by the power of the Holy Spirit (Lk 1:35), she who kept Jesus in her womb for nine months, who fed Jesus in her womb, and later at her breasts. How blessed is Mary who listened to Jesus (Jn 2:4-5), and how blessed is Mary who stood near the Cross of Jesus (19:25-27) when he was creating a new family, that is to say, creating the community of believers, of which Mary becomes the mother (Jn 2:25-27).

To Jesus Through Mary

FR. AZAM - MY PARENTS' WEDDING RING

When I became a priest, my mother gave me a gold ring - a kind of wedding ring. The beauty of that ring was not only that it was made out of gold, but that it was of great importance to my parents. When my father passed away, my mother took his ring and kept it with her. When my eldest brother got married, my mother did not give him that ring; when my second eldest brother got married, my mother did not give him that ring; and when my youngest sister got married, my mother did not give her that ring either.

But when I got became a priest, she took her wedding ring and my father's wedding ring and put them together to make one ring and give it to me. (Since you already know that my mother never gives anything to her children without giving a lesson, so it happened!!!). She gave me the ring and told me, "Now that you are a priest, I want to give you our wedding rings, not only as a gift, but as a reminder." She told me that every rose has a thorn, so too in a marriage! I can say, that day I learned the theology of a wedding ring from my mother.

She told me to spell **RING**. As an obedient child - I did it. After that she continued saying, "This is not only a wedding ring. Remember, Azam, when you wear it - you are embracing - SUFFE**RING**. The suffering does not mean that you should run from it, but you start BEA**RING**. When you start bearing suffering, don't let your life enter into being BO**RING**. When life becomes boring, you begin WONDE**RING** what is going on. Then once again, look at the **RING** and remember, you are putting this **RING** on for CA**RING** for others; SHA**RING** your life with others; and PERSEVE**RING** in your priestly vocation."

✟ ✟ ✟

ABOUT SAINT JOHN EUDES

Born in France on November 14, 1601, St. John Eudes' life spanned the "Great Century." The Age of Discovery had revolutionized technology and exploration; the Council of Trent initiated a much-needed reform in the Church; among the common people, it was the dawn of a golden age of sanctity and mystic fervor.

HIS SPIRITUAL HERITAGE

No fewer than seven Doctors of the Church had lived in the previous century. Great reformers like St. Francis de Sales, St. Teresa of Avila, and St. John of the Cross had left an indelible mark on the Catholic faith. Their influence was still fresh, as St. John Eudes came onto the scene.

He was educated by the Jesuits in rural Normandy. He was ordained into the Oratory of Jesus and Mary, a society of priests which had just been founded on the model of St. Philip Neri's Oratory in Rome. The founder was Cardinal Pierre de Bérulle, a man renowned for his holiness and named "the apostle of the Incarnate Word" by Pope Urban VII. Rounding out St. John Eudes' heritage is the influence of the Discalced Carmelites. His spiritual director, Cardinal Bérulle himself, had brought sisters from St. Teresa of Avila's convent to help found the Carmel in France. John Eudes would later become spiritual director to a Carmelite convent himself. Their cloister prayed constantly for his missionary activity.

HIS LIFE OF MINISTRY

As an avid participant in a wave of re-evangelization in France, St. John Eudes' principal apostolate was preaching parish missions. Spending anywhere from 4 to 20 weeks in each parish, he preached over 120 missions across his lifetime, always with a team of confessors providing the sacrament around the clock, and catechists meeting daily with small groups of parishioners.

Early in his priesthood, an outbreak of plague hit St. John Eudes' native region, and he rushed to provide sacraments to the dying. The risk of contagion was so great that no one else dared to approach the victims. In order to protect his Oratorian brothers from contagion, St. John Eudes took up residence in a large empty cider barrel outside of the city walls until the plague ended.

HIS FOUNDATIONS

During his missions he heard countless confessions himself, including those from women forced into prostitution. Realizing that they needed intense healing and support, he began to found "Houses of Refuge" to help them get off the street and begin a new life. In 1641 he founded the Sisters of Our Lady of Charity of the Refuge to continue this work. They would live with the penitent women and provide them with constant support. Today, these sisters are known as the Good Shepherd Sisters, inspired by their fourth vow of zeal to go out seeking the "lost sheep."

Occasionally, St. John Eudes would return to the site of a previous mission. To his dismay, he found that the fruits of the mission were consistently fading for lack of support. The crucial piece in need of change was the priesthood. At that time, the only way to be trained as a priest was through apprenticeship. The result of this training was so horribly inconsistent that the term "hocus pocus" was invented during this time to describe the corrupted Latin used by poorly trained priests during the consecration at mass. In 1643, he left the Oratory and founded the Congregation of Jesus and Mary to found a seminary. Seminary training was a radical and brand-new concept which had just been proposed by the Council of Trent.

HIS MARK ON THE CHURCH

At a mission in 1648, St. John Eudes celebrated the first mass in history in honor of the Heart of Mary. In 1652, he built the first church under the Immaculate Heart's patronage: the chapel of his seminary in Coutances, France. During the process of his canonization, Pope St. Pius X named St. John Eudes "the father, doctor, and apostle of liturgical devotion to the hearts of Jesus and Mary." The Heart of Jesus, because he also celebrated the first Feast of the Sacred Heart in 1672, just one year before St. Margaret Mary Alacoque had her first apparition of the Sacred Heart.

Although his Marian devotion was intense from a tender age, the primary inspiration for this feast came from St. John Eudes' theology of baptism. From the beginning of his missionary career he taught that Jesus continues His Incarnation in the life of each baptized Christian. As we give ourselves to Christ, our hands become His hands, our hearts are transformed into His heart. Mary is the ultimate exemplar of this. She gave her heart to God so completely that she and Jesus have just one heart between them. Thus, whoever sees Mary, sees Jesus, and honoring the heart of Mary is never separate from honoring the heart of Jesus.

DOCTOR OF THE CHURCH?

At the time of this writing, Bishops the world over have requested that the Vatican proclaim St. John Eudes as a Doctor of the Church. This would recognize his unique contribution to our understanding of the Gospel, and his exemplary holiness of life which stands out even among saints. For more information on the progress of this cause, on his writings or spirituality, or to sign up for our e-newsletter updates, contact spirituality@eudistsusa.org.

ABOUT THE EUDIST FAMILY

During his lifetime, St. John Eudes' missionary activity had three major areas of focus.

- For priests, he provided formation, education, and the spiritual support which is crucial for their role in God's plan of salvation.
- For prostitutes and others on the margins of society, he gave them a home and bound their wounds, like the Good Shepherd with his lost sheep.
- For the laity, he preached the dignity of their baptism and their responsibility to be the hands and feet of God, to continue the Incarnation.

In everything he did, he burned with the desire to be a living example of the love and mercy of God.

These are the "family values" which continue to inspire those who continue his work. To paraphrase St. Paul, John Eudes planted seeds, which others watered through the institutions he founded, and God gave the growth. Today, the family tree continues to bear fruit:

The *Congregation of Jesus and Mary* (CJM), also known as The Eudists, continues the effort to form and care for priests and other leaders within the Church. St. John Eudes called this the mission of "teaching the teachers, shepherding the shepherds, and enlightening those who are the light of the world." Continuing his efforts as a missionary preacher, Eudist priests and brothers "audaciously seek to open up new avenues for evangelization," through television, radio, and new media.

The *Religious of the Good Shepherd* (RGS) continue outreach to women in diffi cult situations, providing them with a deeply needed place of refuge and healing while they seek new lives. St. Mary Euphrasia drastically expanded the reach of this mission, which now operates in over 70 countries worldwide. A true heiress of St. John Eudes, St. Mary Euphrasia exhorted her sisters: "We must go after the lost sheep with no other rest than the cross, no other consolation than work, and no other thirst than for justice."

In every seminary and House of Refuge founded by St. John Eudes, he also established a *Confraternity of the Holy Heart of Jesus and Mary* for the laity, now known as the Eudist Associates. The mission he gave them was twofold: First, "To glorify the divine Hearts of Jesus and Mary... working to make them live and reign in their own heart through diligent imitation of their virtues." Second, "To work for the salvation of souls... by practicing, according to their abilities, works of charity and mercy and by attaining numerous graces through prayer for the clergy and other apostolic laborers."

The *Little Sisters of the Poor* were an outgrowth of this confraternity. St. Jeanne Jugan was formed as a consecrated woman within the Eudist Family. She discovered the great need for love and mercy among the poor and elderly, and the mission took on a life of its own. She passed on to them the Eudist intuition that the poor are not simply recipients of charity, they provide an encounter with Charity Himself: "My little ones, never forget that the poor are Our Lord... In serving the aged, it is He Himself whom you are serving."

A more recent "sprout" on the tree was founded by Mother Antonia Brenner in Tijuana, Mexico. After raising her children in Beverly Hills and suffering through divorce, she followed God's call to become a live-in prison minister at the *La Mesa* penitentiary. The *Eudist Servants of the 11th Hour* was founded so that other women in the latter part of their lives could imitate her in "being love" to those most in need.

The example St. John Eudes set for living out the Gospel has inspired many more individuals and organizations throughout the world. For more information about the Eudist family, news on upcoming publications, or for ways to share in our mission, contact us at spirituality@eudistsusa.org.

About the Eudist Family

ABOUT THE AUTHOR

Fr. Azam Vianney Mansha, CJM belongs to the Congregation of Jesus and Mary, also known as the Eudist Fathers. He is the first Eudist priest from Pakistan. He holds a Pontifical Degree in Sacred Scripture along with degrees from Melbourne School of Divinity, Australia and the Pontifical Urbana University, Rome. He has served as a faculty member and thesis advisor in different theological schools in the Philippines. He is currently serving at St. Patrick Parish, Carlsbad, CA and conducting Bible Studies and Parish Missions in several parishes of the Dioceses of San Diego & San Bernardino.

ENDNOTES

CHAPTER 1: TO JESUS THROUGH MARY

[1] Daniel Sargent, *Their Hearts Be Praised: The Life of Saint John Eudes* (New York: P. J. Kenedy & Sons, 1949), 147-48.

[2] Pierre de Brulle a was sophisticated theologian and aristocrat who served in the French court as royal chaplain. Pope Urban VIII named him a cardinal during the Consistory on 30 August 1627. In 1611, Berulle founded the French Oratory inspired by the Italian Oratory of St. Philip Neri. They were both communities of priests without vows, engaged in a ministry of preaching, education, and the improvement of standards for the clerical state. In 1614, he was appointed by the pope to be canonical superior of the Carmelite nuns in France. He died on October 2nd, 1629. He is also known as the founder of the French School of Spirituality. Pope Urban VIII named him, "The apostle of the Incarnate Word." For further studies, see, William M. Thompson (ed.), *Berulle and the French School: Selected Writings*, translated by Lowell M. Glendon (New York: Paulist Press, 1989), 15-21; Raymond Deville, *The French School of Spirituality: An Introduction and Reader*, translated by Agnes Cunningham (Pittsburgh, Pennsylvania: Duquesne University Press, 1987), 29-57; and Philip Sheldrake, *Spirituality: A Brief History*, 2nd edition (Oxford: Wiley-Blackwell, 2013), 137-40.

[3] John Eudes, *Letters and Shorter Works*, translated by Ruth Hauser (New York: P. J. Kenedy & Sons, 1948), 290-91.

[4] The society was composed of women who lacked the health and condition to enter religious life. The women wore a hidden habit under their ordinary attire: a white scapular in honor of the Immaculate Conception, a white sash in honor of her virginity, and a red cross sewn on the scapular over the heart as symbol of Our Lady's sufferings. Marie des Vallees was likely the first member of this society. For a brief review, see, Daniel Sargent, *Their Hearts Be Praised*, 147-48.

[5] For the development and historical significance of the liturgical feast in honor of the Immaculate Heart of the Blessed Virgin Mary and St. John Eudes' contribution, see, Azam Vianney Mansha, https://www.academia.edu/40935068/THE_HISTORICAL_ SIGNIFICANCE_AND_DEVELOPMENT_OF_THE_LITURGICAL_FEAST_ IN_THE_HONOR_OF_THE_IMMACULATE_HEART_OF_THE_BLESSED_ VIRGIN_MARY_AND_ST._JOHN_EUDES_CONTRIBUTION

[6] Daniel Sargent, *Their Hearts Be Praised*, 1-5.

[7] John Eudes, *Letters and Shorter Works*, 287-88.

[8] Ibid, 287.

[9] Ibid, 301.

[10] Ibid, 177. For St. John Eudes, asking Mary "to show yourself a mother" is a plea to enter into the Marian school where one can learn from her to know Jesus. For comprehensive treatment of this approach, see, Azam Vianney Mansha, https://www.academia.edu/39211873/AN_APPROACH_TO_UNDERSTANDING_THE_MARIAN_SCHOOL_ACCORDING_TO_ST._JOHN_EUDES_IN_THE_LIGHT_OF_AN_EXEGESIS_OF_JOHN_19_25-27. For a brief overview, see also Paul Milcent, *Saint John Eudes: Presentation & Selected Texts* (Glasgow: John S. Burns & Sons, 1964), 127-29.

[11] Daniel Sargent, *Their Hearts Be Praised*, 62-63.

[12] John Eudes, *Letters and Shorter Works*, 295.

[13] Paul Milcent, *Saint John Eudes*, 52.

[14] Daniel Sargent, *Their Hearts Be Praised*, 69.

[15] John Eudes, *Letters and Shorter Works*, 294.

[16] Daniel Sargent, *Their Hearts Be Praised*, 73-5. See also, Raymond Deville, *The French School of Spirituality*, 112-14 and Paul Milcent, *Saint John Eudes*, 10-14.

[17] John Eudes, *Letters and Shorter Works*, 296.

[18] The Heart of Mary is the principle theme in Eudist Mariology. St. John Eudes promoted devotion to the Immaculate Heart of Mary. On his contribution and its historical background, see Azam Vianney Mansha, https://www.academia.edu/39212030/THE_HEART_OF_MARY_THE_PRINCIPLE_THEME_IN_EUDIST_MARIOLOGY. For a recent presentation on the meaning and liturgical celebration of the feast of the Heart of Mary, see, Luc Crepy and Marie-Françoise Le Brizaut, "The Liturgical Celebration of the Heart of Mary," in *Saint John Eudes: Missionary-Priest (1601-1680), Worker for the New Evangelization in the XVII Century*. Translated from French by Anne Josephine Carr and edited by Mary James Wilson (Quezon City: Claretian Communication Foundations, 2016), 101 -106. See also, Jan G. Bovenmars, *A Biblical Spirituality of the Heart* (Alba House, New York, 1991), 160-61 and Paul Milcent, *Saint John Eudes*, 125-29.

[19] John Eudes, *The Admirable Heart of Mary*, translated by Charles di Targiani and Ruth Hauser (New York, 1948), 333.

[20] Daniel Sargent, *Their Hearts Be Praised*, 117.

[21] John Eudes, "Memoriale Beneficiorum Dei" no. 105 in *Letters and Shorter Works*, 314.

Endnotes

[22] John Eudes, *The Admirable Heart of Mary*, xvii-xviii.

[23] John Eudes, *Letters and Shorter Works*, 307.

[24] Daniel Sargent, *Their Hearts Be Praised*, 76. An updated rendition is used here.

[25] Ibid, 199-200.

[26] In the era of St. John Eudes, a parish mission sought to literally re-evangelize a whole region. During this spiritual activity local business stopped and the markets were closed. Processions in the honor of Blessed Sacrament were organized. Priests preached daily for hours on end. A dozen or more priests were present to hear confessions. A special ceremony was organized to burn sinful books and obscene pictures; St. John Eudes called this bonfire a 'fire of joy.' A mission lasted at least one month, but often even longer. For a brief overview, see, Daniel Sargent, *Their Hearts Be Praised*, 40-43.

[27] For a brief reflection on this statue, See, Azam *Vianney* Mansha, https://www.academia.edu/40924040/EUDIST_TRADITIONAL_MARIAN_IMAGE_HISTORY_AND_REFLECTION

[28] Robert de Pas, *Marie, Icone de Jésus: textes de Saint Jean Eudes*, 14. Author's translation of the original French: *"Petite statue en bois stuqué et polychrome. Cette statue appartenait à saint Jean Eudes; elle était sur sa table, et il l'emportait parfois dans ses missions."*

[29] See, Alvaro Torres, *St. Jean Eudes: A Priest according to the Heart of God*, translated by Lizanne Marsh (N. C: Rodek Print, N.Y), 39-40.

[30] John Eudes, *Letters and Shorter Works*, 300-302.

[31] For a brief overview about Eudes' trials, see, Daniel Sargent, *Their Hearts Be Praised*, 166-194; Alvaro Torres, *St. Jean Eudes: A Priest according to the Heart of God*, " The Cross of Christ," 20-22; "A Door Closes," 26-27; "Difficulties in Our Lady of Charity," 32-33 and "Troubles on the Way," 37-38 and Paul Milcent, *Saint John Eudes*, 18-20.

[32] John Eudes, *Letters and Shorter Works*, 303.

[33] Ibid, 318-323.

[34] John Eudes, *Oeuvres Completes I*, 432-433. All the English translation is taken from Louis Levesque, *Lectionary Proper to the Congregation of Jesus and Mary*, 1989.

[35] John Eudes, *Letters and Shorter Works*, 325-330, 327.

[36] Ibid, 338-39. Author's translation of the original Latin: *"O clemens, O pia, O dulcis Virgo Maria, vita, dulcedo et spes mea charissima."*

[37] Alvaro Torres, *St. Jean Eudes: A Priest according to the Heart of God*, 48-49.

CHAPTER 2: TO JESUS THROUGH MARY
- TURNING TOWARD MARY -

[38] For an overview on the principle theological themes in the French School of Spirituality, see, Azam Vianney Mansha, https://www.academia.edu/38058140/THE_THEOLOGY_OF_THE_FRENCH_SCHOOL_OF_SPIRITUALITY.

[39] The author has reviewed: Cardinal Pierre de Berulle, John-Jacques Olier, John Eudes, and Louis de Montfort in relation to their contribution in Mariology. For Cardinal Pierre de Berulle, Jean-Jacques Olier and John Eudes, see, Raymond Deville, *The French School of Spirituality: An Introduction and Reader.* Translated by Agnes Cunningham (Pittsburgh, Pennsylvania: Duquesne University Press, 1994).

[40] For a recent presentation on the meaning and liturgical celebration of this feast, see, Luc Crepy and Marie-Françoise Le Brizaut, "The Liturgical Celebration of the Heart of Mary," in *Saint John Eudes: Missionary-Priest (1601-1680), Worker for the New Evangelization in the XVII Century*, 101-106.

[41] For an overview on the historical development of the feast of Immaculate Heart of the Blessed Virgin Mary, see, Azam Vianney Mansha, *The Historical Significance and Development of the Liturgical Feast in the Honor of the Immaculate Heart of the Blessed Virgin Mary*, https://www.academia.edu/40935068/THE_HISTORICAL_SIGNIFICANCE_AND_DEVELOPMENT_OF_THE_LITURGICAL_FEAST_IN_THE_HONOR_OF_THE_IMMACULATE_HEART_OF_THE_BLESSED_VIRGIN_MARY_AND_ST_JOHN_EUDES_CONTRIBUTION

[42] The English translation is taken from Louis Levesque, *Lectionary Proper to the Congregation of Jesus and Mary*, 1989.

[43] John Eudes, *The Admirable Heart of Mary*, xvii.

[44] Pius X, Apostolic Letter for the Beatification of Ven. John Eudes (April 11, 1909), *Acta Apostolicae Sedis* (Rome, 1909): 480.

[45] John Eudes, *The Admirable Heart of Mary*, 9.

[46] For an overview on Augustian Mariology, see, Azam Vianney Mansha, https://www.academia.edu/38045363/An_attempt_to_understand_Augustian_Mariology

[47] John Eudes, *Oeuvres Complétes* VII, 245.

[48] John Eudes, *Oeuvres Complétes* VIII, 429.

[49] John Eudes, *Oeuvres Complétes* VII, 279.

[50] John Eudes, *Oeuvres Complétes* VIII, 461

[51] John Eudes, *Oeuvres Complétes* I, 432-433.

[52] John Eudes, *The Admirable Heart of Mary*, 3.

Endnotes

CHAPTER 3: THE MARIAN SCHOOL

[53] John Eudes, *Admirable Heart of Mary*, xvii.

[54] For a recent presentation on the meaning and liturgical celebration of this feast, see, Luc Crepy and Marie- Françoise Le Brizaut, "The Liturgical Celebration of the Heart of Mary," in *Saint John Eudes: Missionary-Priest (1601-1680), Worker for the New Evangelization in the XVII Century*, 101 -106.

[55] John Eudes, *The Admirable Heart of Mary*, 3.

[56] John Paul II, *Redemptoris Mater* [The Mother of the Redeemer]. Vatican City: Vatican Press, 1987, paragraph # 26. https://www.vatican.va/content/john-paul-ii/en/encyclicals/documents/hf_jp-ii_enc_25031987_redemptoris-mater.html.

[57] John Rotelle, O.S.A., ed., "Sermon 187.1: On Christmas Day: The greatness and the humility of Christ," in *The Works of Saint Augustine: A translation for the 21st Century*, Sermons III/6: on the Liturgical Seasons trans. Edmund Hill, O.P., (New York: New City Press, 1993), 27.

[58] John Eudes, *Oeuvres Complètes* VII, 461 & 114.

[59] Interestingly, the proper name of the Mother of Jesus is never mentioned in the Gospel of John. Indeed, John's failure to use the personal name of the Mother of Jesus is striking because John is not shy of that name. The proper name "Mary" almost occurs fifteen times in the Gospel: for Mary the sister of Martha, for Mary Magdalene, for Mary the wife of Clopas. For this study, the personal name of the Mother of Jesus, Mary, is adopted from the Synoptics.

[60] See Azam Vianney Mansha, "'The Mother of Jesus,' 'His Mother,' and 'The Woman,' An Attempt to Understand Johannine Mariology" (STL thesis, Loyola School of Theology, 2017), 70-71.

[61] Veronica Koperski "The Mother of Jesus and Mary Magdalene: Looking Back and Forward from the Foot of the Cross in John 19,25-27," in *The Death of Jesus in the Fourth Gospel* (Leuven: Leuven University, 2007):849-58, 856.

[62] See Craig R. Koester, *Symbolism in the Fourth Gospel* (Minneapolis: Fortress Press, 2003), 240-41.

[63] See John Kurichiyaniyil, "Mary in the Gospel of John," *BB 371/1* (March 2011):42-73, 68.

[64] See C. K. Barrett, *The Gospel According to St. John: An Introduction with Commentary and Notes on the Greek Text*, 2d ed. (London: SPCK, 1978) 459. See also M. de Goedt, "Un schème de révélation dans le quatrième évangile," *NTS* 8 (1961-62):142-150.

[65] See, Moloney, *The Gospel of John*, Sacra Pagina Series vol. 4, edited by Daniel J. Harrington (Collegeville, Minnesota: Liturgial Press, 1998), 504.

[66] Andre Feuillet, *Jesus and His Mother: The Role of the Virgin Mary in Salvation History and the Place of Woman in the Church*, trans. Leonard Maluf (Massachusetts: St. Bede's Pub., 1984), 9

[67] Robert de Pas, *Marie, Icone de Jésus: textes de Saint Jean Eudes* (n.d. & n.p.), 14.

www.ingramcontent.com/pod-product-compliance
Lightning Source LLC
Chambersburg PA
CBHW060035180426
43196CB00045B/2691